The 60 Minute Financial Guide

How to Thrive in Your 20s and Beyond

Terry Zavitz, CFP, CLU, CHS, GBA, EPC

&

Justine Zavitz, CFP, CHS, CLU

The 60-Minute Financial Guide
140319-003

Published by:
90-Minute Books
Newinformation Inc
302 Martinique Drive
Winter Haven, FL 33884
www.90minutebooks.com

ISBN-13: 978-1508553236
ISBN-10: 1508553238

For more information on 90-Minute Books including finding out how you can publish your own lead generating book, visit www.90minutebook.com or call (863) 318-0464.

Here's What's Inside...

Introduction

The 60 Minute Financial Guide – How to Thrive in Your 20s and Beyond

Over the last 30 years, while assisting clients with their insurance and financial planning needs we often hear people in their 40s say, "If I had known this beforehand, I would be far better off!"

Conversely, some of our younger clients who are in their 20s often express a very different sentiment; "I don't have a lot of money, so I don't have to worry about what to do with it."

There is no question that establishing strong financial habits and avoiding common financial pitfalls will result in greater wealth and financial stability over your lifetime. In fact, this is often more important than how much money you make.

Finishing school and establishing a career with a decent salary can be a challenge. We want you to enjoy your financial successes without sacrificing your long-term goals. To help guide you, we've compiled a list of 10 common financial hazards you may encounter, as well as tips on how to avoid them.

We hope this book educates you and encourages you to begin laying the foundation of your financial road map, which is the key to a solid financial future. These 10 tips will help you to thrive financially in your 20s and beyond.

To Your Success!

Terry Zavitz & Justine Zavitz

Chapter 1: Different Levels of Poor

Clients in their 20s often believe that their financial situation will become easier once they are finished school and start making an income. Sometimes this is the case; however we've learned that more often than not, they just experience "different levels of poor."

What do we mean by this? Allow us to use James as an example. James was in university and living on a fixed budget with an income of $15,000 per year. In order to live on that income, he chose Netflix over cable, a pay-as-you-go phone plan, and drank the cheap beer. After graduation James started to make more money. He was now earning $50,000 a year as an Account Manager in Montreal. He switched to cable, upgraded to the latest iPhone, bought a car, moved into a nicer apartment and developed a taste for imported beer. Despite his increased income, at the end of the month he had very little left over. This is what we refer to as a "different level of poor."

It is a myth that living within your means becomes easier once you start making more money. The reality is, the more you make, the more you spend. This is because typically once you make more money your standard of living increases. No matter how much you earn, you continue to struggle with financial constraints. Despite the growth of your income, you will always be faced with financial challenges, although they may present themselves in various forms.

It is important is to review your budget frequently, make decisions based on your current means, and set your financial goals accordingly, rather than putting off savings or going into debt.

Tip #1: Live within your current means rather than what you anticipate your future means will be.

Chapter 2: Caution! There Are Taxes Ahead

Sarah recently graduated from college and has been hired as a graphic designer in Toronto with a salary of $41,000. While in school she managed to live on a budget of $18,000 a year, which was provided for by student loans and assistance from her parents. She is excited that her income is doubling and is making plans for all of this extra money.

Even though Sarah thinks she is doubling her income, she will only take home about $900 a month more.

Here's why...

Sarah's income as a student was not subject to tax since loans and gifts from parents are not considered income for tax purposes. However, her income as a graphic designer will be subject to tax, along with other statutory deductions (Canada Pension Plan, Employment Insurance contributions), which will reduce the amount of income she takes home. Since Sarah is an employee, taxes and deductions will be deducted directly from her pay. The chart below illustrates the impact that taxes have on your gross income.

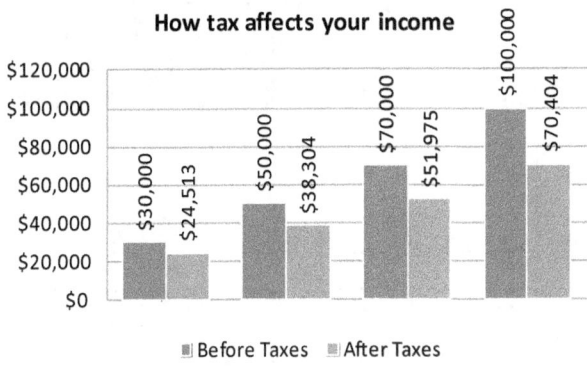

How tax affects your income

$120,000
$100,000
$80,000
$60,000
$40,000
$20,000
$0

$30,000 $24,513 $50,000 $38,304 $70,000 $51,975 $100,000 $70,404

■ Before Taxes ■ After Taxes

*This chart assumes no RRSP contributions were made.

In Canada we have a graduated tax rate system. This means that the higher the income, the greater the percentage of taxes owed. Your *marginal* tax rate is the highest tax bracket that you fall within. Your *average* tax rate is the overall tax percentage versus your income.

We've included a chart outlining the top marginal tax rates on different incomes for residents of Ontario.

Combined Federal & Ontario Tax Brackets and Tax Rates Including Surtaxes									
	2015 Marginal Tax Rates					2014 Marginal Tax Rates			
2015 Taxable Income	Income	Capital Gains	Canadian Dividends		2014 Taxable Income	Income	Capital Gains	Canadian Dividends	
			Eligible	Non-Eligible				Eligible	Non-Eligible
first $40,922	20.05%	10.03%	-6.86%	5.35%	first $40,120	20.05%	10.03%	-6.86%	5.35%
over $40,922 up to $44,701	24.15%	12.08%	-1.20%	10.19%	over $40,120 up to $43,953	24.15%	12.08%	-1.20%	10.19%
over $44,701 up to $72,064	31.15%	15.58%	8.46%	18.45%	over $43,953 up to $70,651	31.15%	15.58%	8.46%	18.45%
over $72,064 up to $81,847	32.98%	16.49%	10.99%	20.61%	over $70,651 up to $80,242	32.98%	16.49%	10.99%	20.61%
over $81,847 up to $84,902	35.39%	17.7%	14.31%	23.45%	over $80,242 up to $83,237	35.39%	17.7%	14.31%	23.45%
over $84,902 up to $89,401	39.41%	19.7%	19.86%	28.19%	over $83,237 up to $87,907	39.41%	19.7%	19.86%	28.19%
over $89,401 up to $138,586	43.41%	21.70%	25.38%	32.91%	over $87,907 up to $136,270	43.41%	21.70%	25.38%	32.91%
over $138,586 up to $150,000	46.41%	23.20%	29.52%	36.45%	over $136,270 up to $150,000	46.41%	23.20%	29.52%	36.45%
over $150,000 to $220,000	47.97%	23.98%	31.67%	38.29%	over $150,000 up to $220,000	47.97%	23.98%	31.67%	38.29%
over $220,000	49.53%	24.76%	33.82%	40.13%	over $220,000	49.53%	24.76%	33.82%	40.13%

Marginal tax rate for dividends is a % of actual dividends received (not grossed-up amount).

Marginal tax rate for capital gains is a % of total capital gains (not taxable capital gains).

Gross-up rate for eligible dividends is 38%, and for non-eligible dividends is 18%.

The surtax is calculated before deducting dividend tax credits.

Marginal tax rates do not include the Ontario Health Premium, which increases the above rates by up to 1.2%

These rates were provided by http://www.taxtips.ca/taxrates/on.htm

For the first $40,120 of Sarah's income, her tax rate is 20.05%, and for the next $880 of income, her tax rate is 24.15%. Sarah's top marginal tax rate is 24.15%. The total tax payable after accounting for tax credits and deductions is $5,852, meaning that her average tax rate is 14.27% ($5852 ÷ $41,000).

Sarah's friend Emily graduated from medical school, completed her residency, and is starting her practice as a family doctor. She expects to make $180,000 this year. Because this money is considered self-employment income and not salaried income, taxes will not be automatically deducted off of her pay. She will have to remit taxes and statutory deductions, such as Canada Pension Plan (CPP), herself. Emily has her accountant estimate the remittances she will have to make and opens a second bank account where she transfers in 1/3 of her income every month. She knows that in her first year of self-employment she will owe the government this money by April of the following year. Every year thereafter she will have to remit estimated taxes and CPP payments on a quarterly basis.

Tip #2: Know your tax rate and plan accordingly.

Chapter 3: To Save or Not to Save? That Is Not the Question

Dan is 27 and has started his career working as a lawyer at a major law firm in town. He is earning $80,000 annually and can live on this income with $1000/month left over which he can contribute to savings or use to pay down debt. He recently got married and plans to purchase a home with his new wife. He also has a student debt of $50,000 at prime, an interest rate that can fluctuate, through a line of credit that he would like to pay off.

Dan's dilemma is common among new graduates, the question of saving or paying down debt. By reducing debt each month, he is able to save interest costs at the prime rate. If this money was directed to his savings instead, Dan needs to earn more than the prime rate in after tax investment returns to equal the benefit of paying down debt. However, if he chooses to contribute to his savings he may run into trouble when interest rates climb and his debt costs increase. But what happens if markets decline and he loses a significant portion of what he has saved? Calculated planning is required with respect to anticipated benefits since some types of savings vehicles will help to reduce his tax bill as he moves into higher brackets, which frees up more money to pay down debt.

Since we can't anticipate the future regarding interest rates or the size of investment returns, let's start by considering the savings vehicles available and how they might help Dan reach his goal of buying a home. The most common savings vehicles are Registered Retirement Savings Plans (RRSP) and Tax Free Savings Accounts (TFSA).

With an RRSP, the maximum amount you can contribute is based on 18% of your previous year's income, to a maximum of $24,930 (in 2015), plus any contribution room you may have accumulated in previous years. The contribution is tax deductible, which means it can be written off to reduce your overall tax bill. The growth from the money invested is tax sheltered, which means you will pay no income tax each year. However, any withdrawals from the plan are 100% taxable as income (with some specific exceptions). Unless you are taking advantage of one of the exceptions (which we will explore next), saving in an RRSP is usually recommended for the long term.

For certain savings needs, such as a down payment for a home, RRSPs are an excellent vehicle because of programs offered by the Government. The *Home Buyers Plan* is one of these programs and allows you to withdraw up to $25,000 from your RRSP tax free to help with the down payment for a house. The money must be paid back over 15 years, and although there is no interest charged, this money does not earn any investment income within the RRSP. If both spouses are new home buyers, each can borrow $25,000.

With a Tax Free Savings Account, you accumulate $5,500 per year in new contribution room (the maximum amount the Government will allow you to deposit). The amount of contributions not made since you became eligible will accrue and can be deposited in future years. Contributions are not tax deductible like an RRSP, but the investment income will grow tax-free. In addition, any amount withdrawn from a TFSA is tax-free. A TFSA does not have the same immediate advantages as an RRSP, but is efficient if you need to retrieve the money at a later date due to the tax-free accumulation of income.

Below is a chart outlining the differences from a tax perspective of an RRSP and TFSA.

TFSA or RRSP?					
	Tax deductible	Tax deferred on growth	No tax on withdrawal	Rules of Withdrawal	Contribution room calculation
TFSA		✓	✓	Can withdraw any amount from the account at any time, tax free	$5,500 per year, + any amounts previously withdrawn in any year. Unused amounts can be accumulated
RRSP	✓	✓		Tax must be paid on any amount withdrawn. Must be converted to a retirement withdrawal plan, such as a RRIF or annuity, by the end of the year you turn age 71	The lesser of 18% of your previous years income; or the maximum limit shown on your Notice of Assessment. Unused amounts can be accumulated and used later

Tax Free Savings Account

- Great for short and long term savings such as emergency funds, vacations, home purchase, retirement etc.
- Popular for people in all tax brackets
- Often better savings vehicle than a RRSP for people in lower tax brackets

Registered Retirement Savings Plan

- Great retirement savings vehicle
- Popular among those in high tax brackets as contributions are tax deductible
- Home Buyers Plan allows first time home buyers to withdraw up to $25,000 tax free for purchase of a home

Dan has some unused RRSP contribution room and, given the fact that he is in the 32% tax bracket, he will get $320 back for every $1,000 contributed (up to a limit) because of the RRSP tax deduction. There is no deduction or money back if he contributes to a TFSA. He can borrow the money from his RRSP in a future year through the Home Buyers Plan and use this money for a down payment. He can also use the tax refund to pay down his student loans. If he contributes the full $12,000 to his RRSP he will have close to $3,800 in tax refunds to assist in paying down his student debt.

If Dan was earning $30,000 with no debt or plans to buy a home and expected his income to increase to $100,000 by the time he is 35, there may be another answer. He would be in the 20% tax bracket now, and would get a tax refund of $200 for every $1,000 invested in an RRSP. He will soon be in the 43% tax bracket. It may be better for him to save within a TFSA for now and later use this money to contribute to an RRSP once he has a higher income and will earn $430 back for every $1,000 invested. He could also contribute to an RRSP now and declare the tax deduction in a future year.

As you can see, the answer to the question of saving versus paying down debt is variable – it depends! Aside from looking at the numbers, tax savings, etc. there are many other considerations. For instance, what is your debt tolerance? Some people just can't stand to be in debt! What is your risk tolerance in the market? How soon do you want to own a home? What is your anticipated income for the future? What are current and expected interest rates and investment returns? A balanced approach of saving and paying down debt is often the best option given that none of us can predict the future. The most important message here is to start saving and pay down debt as soon as possible and make it a habit. At the end of the day, if your net worth is increasing, it is a sign that you are doing the right thing.

TIP #3: Start saving early and understand the savings options and the tax benefits available.

Chapter 4: Budget Isn't a Bad Word

Budgeting…blah! It sounds like a chore to create a budget and even more tedious to stick to it. Let's face it, it is a lot more fun to spend money as we earn it, but of course, this is not financially prudent. Without implementing a budget, you may find yourself unable to pay your rent and could end up having to move back into your parents' house! You could also find yourself in debt for the rest of your life, making your retirement goals difficult to achieve. We dread having to tell our clients that they have to work another 10 years beyond their desired retirement age because they failed to budget earlier in life.

So what's the best way to budget? Let's take a look at Jessica's situation.

Jessica has been working for 5 years and is currently earning $70,000 a year as a dental hygienist. Despite the fact she is making a decent salary, Jessica is struggling with paying down her debt. She enjoys dining out 2 or 3 times a week and loves to go shopping on weekends. These habits leave her only enough money to pay the minimum monthly payments on her line of credit, which takes care of interest costs without reducing the principal. Jessica wonders what needs to be done in order to more efficiently pay off her debt and allow her to save some money, purchase a condo and do some travelling.

As your income increases, it is all too easy to upgrade your lifestyle and find yourself "broke" again without the means to save or accomplish other financial goals. Jessica can take concrete steps to solve her debt elimination problem by taking a good look at where she is spending her money. There are some great websites and applications to help with this. The simplest way to figure out her after-tax income and monthly expenses is to use a website like *Mint.com.* It will allow her to export information from her bank account and credit card statements, categorizing them into easy to read charts. Jessica could also use her online banking system to export monthly statements to Excel and sort them herself. Most importantly, Jessica has to recognize the discrepancy between wants and needs. Once she knows how much she is spending, she can eliminate or reduce unnecessary expenses and determine what she needs to live on each month. The excess can be allocated to debt repayment. To make sure these payments happen she can set up automatic transfers every payday.

Jessica also needs to know which debts she should pay first. Typically the best order to repay your debt is:

1. Non- deductible high interest rate debt (e.g. Credit cards)

2. Non-deductible low interest debt (e.g. mortgage, line of credit or low interest car payment)

3. Deductible high interest debt (e.g. corporate credit card)

4. Deductible low interest debt (e.g. corporate line of credit)

Jessica has a student loan of $10,000 with an annual interest payment of 5%, or $500, which is considered a non-deductible low interest debt. Student loans are not deductible unless they come from a special government program. In Ontario, OSAP loans receive a tax credit, which effectively reduces the overall interest rate being paid; however, these rates can still be higher than what the bank is offering despite the tax savings.

The importance of having a budget cannot be overemphasized.

Tip #4: Create a realistic budget and stick to it.

Chapter 5: Compound Interest - The Good, The Bad & The Ugly

Michael inherited $100,000 from his grandfather and is looking for a secure long- term investment. He knows the bank offers GIC's (Guaranteed Investment Certificates) at 3% compound or 3.5% simple interest. The 3.5% interest rate seems like the right choice to Michael since it's higher. However, to make this decision he needs to know the difference between simple and compound interest.

Simple interest pays a percentage of the original amount invested each year. For Michael, this would be $3,500 a year.

Compound interest pays a percentage of interest on the total balance, which means it allows for earning interest on the interest. Using Michael as our example, he would earn $3,000 the first year and $3,090 the second year. Even though the interest payments start out lower, by year 7, he would earn $3,582. By year 13, the cumulative investment from compound interest surpasses that of the cumulative investment from simple interest and it will continue to grow by more. By year 30, the compound investment has outperformed the simple interest investment by over $34,000.

To illustrate the difference between simple and compound interest, the chart below compares 3% compound interest vs 3.5% simple interest for a $1,000 investment over a 40 year period.

Compound Interest vs. Simple Interest

Compound Interest	Yr 1 – 10	Yr 10 - 20	Yr 20 - 30	Yr 30 – 40
Opening balance	$1,000	$1,344	$1,806	$2,427
Cumulative Interest earned during period assuming 3% compound interest	$344	$468	$621	$835
End of period balance	$1,344	$1,806	$2,427	$3,262

Simple Interest	Yr 1 – 10	Yr 10 – 20	Yr 20 – 30	Yr 30 – 40
Opening balance	$1,000	$1,350	$1,700	$2,050
Cumulative Interest earned during period assuming 3.5% simple interest	$350	$350	$350	$350
Closing balance	$1,350	$1,700	$2,050	$2,400

Compound interest has been touted as the 8th Wonder of the World when it comes to investment returns; however, it works in reverse when interest compounds on money you owe. Your debt can become much larger if adequate payments are not made as interest costs grow on top of interest costs. Compound interest makes your debt grow exponentially faster, see the chart below.

How Compound Interest Affects Debt					
	Year 1	Year 3	Year 5	Year 10	Year 15
Debt owing at start of the year	$5,000	$5,512.50	$6,077.53	$7,756.64	$9,899.66
Interest Rate	5%	5%	5%	5%	5%
Payment made during the year	0	0	0	0	0
Debt owing at end of the year	$5,250	$5,788.13	$6,381.41	$8,144.47	$10,394.64
Total Interest Accumulated	$250	$788.13	$1,381.41	$3,144.47	$5,394.64

Tip #5: Compound interest is a blessing when you are investing and a curse when you borrow if the interest is not paid.

Chapter 6: The Mortgage Factor

A mortgage is quite likely the largest debt you will ever have. The good news is that it's considered "good debt," because it helps build equity and your net worth. Before you decide to take on a debt of this magnitude, there are a number of things you need to do in preparation.

Let's look at the examples of two couples that both have decided they would like to buy homes – David and Megan, and Marty and Donna.

David earns $50,000 a year as a programmer and his girlfriend Megan earns the same as an executive assistant. They have figured out what they can afford in housing costs each month, while continuing to accomplish their other financial goals. They have reviewed their total monthly expenses, anticipated property taxes in their desired neighbourhood, as well as extra costs for regular maintenance and upkeep, which is estimated at 3-5% of the value of their home each year.

Marty and Donna earn the same incomes as David and Megan. Instead of determining their own monthly budget, they went to the bank to ask how much mortgage they qualify for. The bank made note of the size of their combined incomes, along with their current debt load in order to come up with the maximum mortgage amount they can get.

These couples have used different approaches to determine their housing budgets and therefore will arrive at different answers. David and Megan have accounted for some of the extra costs involved in owning their own home and have included their other financial goals in their budget. On the flip side, Marty and Donna are only basing the amount of money they will spend on a house on the maximum mortgage the bank will approve, which is often higher. When other costs are added, it is likely Marty and Donna will be "house poor", meaning they will not have any extra money to pay down other debts, go on vacations or achieve other financial goals.

David and Megan decide to speak to their banker. The banker explains that they are eligible to borrow $350,000 for a mortgage, which is more than they had decided to spend. They share their budget with their banker, which prompts a discussion on the value of a down payment and the possibility of added fees, called CMHC fees, in the event the down payment is too small.

Canada Mortgage & Housing Corporation (CMHC) is loan default insurance for banks that is mandatory when homebuyers make down payments less than 20% of the value of the house. The premiums are charged at a graduated rate, depending on the amount of the down payment, and are added to the monthly mortgage payments. The chart below outlines the impact of these fees on a monthly payment.

CMHC Costs on $100,000 Home Purchase

	Assumptions	5% Down Payment	20% Down Payment
Purchase Price		$100,000	$100,000
Less: Down Payment		5% = $ 5,000	20% = $20,000
Amount to Finance		$95,000	$80,000
Add: CMHC Insurance	3.15%*	$2,992	$0.00
Mortgage Amount		$97,992	$80,000
Monthly Payment**	4.94%***	$566.58	$462.56

*Based on published CMHC rates August, 2014
**Assuming monthly payments amortized over 25 years
***Based on RBC posted 5 year Fixed Rate August, 2014
Numbers have been rounded to nearest dollar

Luckily, David and Megan are financially prudent and have already started saving in their RRSPs and TFSAs, accumulating $60,000 so far. They can buy a $300,000 house without incurring CMHC fees. The mortgage amount would be $240,000, which falls within their budget.

Marty and Donna realize the amount of mortgage they were approved for might be too high after doing a budget exercise. In addition, their banker has explained the added cost of CMHC fees with a down payment of less than 20%. Marty and Donna have saved only $20,000. Based on the size of house they want to buy, CMHC fees are inevitable. They will have to decide if they want to save for a few more years to accumulate more savings or buy the house now and pay the fees. If they choose to buy the house now, the added fees will impact their total monthly expenses, which will impact the value of the house they can afford.

Along with deciding what purchase price is affordable to pay for their home, the two couples need to consider the *amortization period*, which is the number of years given to pay the mortgage off. The shorter the amortization period, the higher the payment; however, with a short amortization period, the mortgage will be paid off sooner with less interest costs incurred. The maximum amortization period is 25 years if you have a CMHC insured mortgage, or 30 years for non-insured mortgages.

The couples also need to consider how frequently they will make payments. The most common are monthly, biweekly or weekly. The more frequent the payments and the shorter the amortization period, the less interest they will pay over the life of the mortgage. The chart below illustrates the difference in monthly payments and total interest costs incurred with different amortization periods and frequency of payments.

250,000 mortgage with Monthly payments

	20 year mortgage	25 year mortgage
Amount financed	$250,000	$250,000
Interest Rate	4%	4%
Monthly Payment	$1,510.62	$1,315.05
Total Interest Paid	$112,547.88	$144,515.15

$250,000 mortgage with Bi-Weekly payments

	20 year mortgage	25 year mortgage
Amount financed	$250,000	$250,000
Interest Rate	4%	4%
Bi-Weekly Payment	$755.00	$658.00
Total Interest Paid	$97,821.00	$123,453.00

There are several mortgage payment calculators available online that can be useful to figure out the appropriate payment options for your individual circumstances.

There are also other expenses that need to be considered when buying a home, including land transfer tax, legal fees, the length of time you plan to stay in the home, and the subsequent costs associated with selling.

TIP #6: Buy a house that fits within your budget and don't forget the extra expenses.

Chapter 7: You Don't Need Superpowers to Protect Yourself Financially

The rule of thumb when it comes to insurance is, "If you can't afford the loss, you need to insure it." This applies in all circumstances, from the extended warranty on your new TV, to insuring your most important asset, your income! There is a great deal to know about the world of insurance, but for now we'll stick to the basics.

Karim and Kayla have been married and working for the past 5 years. They have one child with a second on the way. They currently have a combined income of $100,000 per year. They own a home, two cars and have $5,000 in savings. Life is good as their incomes are growing along with their net worth. Karim and Kayla don't have any health issues. What kinds of insurance would be appropriate for this happy couple?

Karim and Kayla need to make sure that their home and cars are properly insured. Imagine the financial impact if they lost their house and contents due to a fire or other disaster. They should speak to a Property and Casualty insurance provider (also known as General Insurance providers), who offer products like car, house and liability insurance. They can also assist with insurance on businesses such as commercial liability, fire and theft, and practice interruption.

Next, Karim and Kayla need to make sure they protect themselves and their family should something unexpected occur from a health perspective. It's common for people under 40 to feel invincible when it comes to their health and they often assume it is unlikely that major health concerns will affect them. They are OK now, and they don't worry about getting sick, becoming disabled or dying. The reality is that this happens all too often!

The financial plans we establish to help clients reach goals are based on the assumption that your income continues in its current form. When you think about it, your ability to earn an income is arguably your greatest asset. Without it, you would not be able to afford your house, car, savings and anything else. After an accident or change in health, it may be too late to get insurance, so getting it as soon as possible, while you're still healthy, is critical.

Karim and Kayla need to make sure they have *disability insurance* to protect their income if they cannot work, *life insurance* to protect their lifestyle should one of them die prematurely, and *critical illness insurance* to protect their cash flow and savings if one of them develops a major illness. They will need to speak to a Life, Accident and Illness insurance broker to seek advice. This type of advisor has a different license than the general insurance provider. It is very common for people to have different insurance brokers to look after their different needs.

When deciding on insurance providers, Karim and Kayla should know the difference between a broker and an agent so they understand their options. Agents typically work for one insurance carrier and offer that company's products. Brokers have contracts with multiple insurance carriers and can shop the marketplace, reviewing the plethora of different products and prices to determine the best solution for their clients. It is important to know what company or companies your advisor represents.

Finding the best contracts and product prices is helpful, but at the end of the day, having a proactive insurance advisor is crucial. It's important that your advisor reaches out to you regularly to review your insurances relative to your circumstances since you will get busy with "life" and may forget to do it yourself. Your advisor's expertise and experience will have an impact on both implementing and claiming on the insurance.

We regularly come in contact with clients who have implemented insurance plans by themselves, often resulting in inadequate and costly coverage. Associations, alumni groups, banks and retail stores often have their own insurance plans available to their members or customers. These plans are not necessarily less expensive or better contractually than what is available on the open market, so it is best to find someone you trust to help you understand all of your options.

Below is a short summary of some of the insurance plans to consider.

Types of Insurance

	What is it?	When do I need it?
Life Insurance*	Provides a lump sum payment of money to a designated beneficiary if the insured person dies while the policy is in force	Any time you have dependents you want to provide for. It also can be used for estate planning later in life.
Disability Insurance*	Provides a monthly benefit if the insured is unable to work due to injury or sickness, and suffers a loss of income	During your working life. This is more comprehensive than WSIB which covers accident on the job or industrial
Critical Illness Insurance*	Pays a lump sum benefit if the insured is diagnosed with an illness covered by the policy contract and survives the waiting period. All policies cover cancer, stroke and heart attack, and 20 other illnesses can be added.	Your entire life, but especially while working. Critical Illness coverage acts as a great supplement to Disability Insurance
Health Insurance*	Supplements provincial and territorial health coverage. Can cover things such as prescription drugs, dental expenses, eye glasses, medical devices, various types of therapy and counseling.	Your entire life.
Home & Tenant Insurance	Home insurance protects the physical house and contents. Tenant insurance protects a tenant's contents in a rented property.	Any time you own a house or rent a property.
Auto Insurance	Insurance purchased to cover costs associated with getting into an automobile accident. May pay for damages to your car, or another person's car or property as well as liability	Required by law when you own a vehicle.
Travel Insurance*	Insurance to cover unexpected costs during domestic and international travel. May cover out of country medical expenses, or costs associated with trip cancellations.	Any time you are travelling.

TIP #7: Do your research and shop around before making any final insurance decisions.

Chapter 8: What You Need to Know About Group Benefits

You may be lucky enough to have access to a group benefits plan through your workplace. Group benefits can be a great way to cover some of your insurance needs with minimal effort and cost.

Elena has been hired as a nurse at the local hospital. Her husband Hassan is still in school completing his engineering degree. Elena has been offered group benefits as part of her overall compensation package, however, is not eligible to join the group benefit plan until her probation period has passed, which is 3 months from her date of hire. At that point, she will have 30 days to enroll herself and her husband without having to submit medical information and provide proof of health. Elena is a diabetic and therefore is considered a higher risk from an insurance perspective. If she does not enroll within the 30-day window, it is likely she will not be eligible for most if not all of the group benefits.

The 30-day enrollment provision also applies to spouses and children. If Elena has a child, she will need to notify the insurance carrier within 30 days of the child's birth and add the child to the plan. If Hassan is a common-law spouse (rather than legally married), he is likely to be eligible for benefits under Elena's plan, providing they meet the definition of a common-law spouse in their respective province (we'll cover this in more detail in the next chapter). Failing to recognize a common-law spouse's eligibility for acceptance into a group benefits plan is a frequent oversight. A common-law spouse must be enrolled in the group benefit plan within 30 days after becoming common-law in order to avoid providing medical evidence. In Ontario, this is defined as living together in a conjugal relationship for 12 consecutive months; however, this definition varies by province. If this deadline is missed, medical evidence is required and the spouse risks being declined. A change in marital status from common-law to legally married does not restart the eligibility period.

The benefits package that Elena's employer offers includes life insurance, short and long term disability insurance, extended health care and dental insurance. Extended health care includes prescription drugs, paramedical practitioners (e.g. chiropractors, physiotherapists, massage therapists), medical supplies (e.g. hearing aids, walkers, canes, and crutches), private duty nursing, and out-of-country travel coverage.

It is important for Elena and Hassan to review the benefits booklet so that they know what they are covered for. The life and disability insurance portion of the plan covers Elena only, as the employee, while the health and dental benefits cover both Elena and Hassan.

The health and dental benefits could have an annual deductible, which is a specified dollar amount that the employee must pay each year before the insurance starts to reimburse these expenses. For example, a $50/year deductible means Elena must pay the first $50 of expenses out of her own pocket. These benefits could also have a coinsurance element, which is a specified percentage that will be reimbursed for each claim. For example, a coinsurance of 80% on dental means 80% of each dental claim will be reimbursed by insurance with the other 20% being paid by Elena. There could be annual maximum limits on certain benefits, such as having massage therapy covered up to $500/year/person.

Long-term disability coverage may have a pre-existing condition clause included, which restricts benefits payable for a certain period of time for health issues that were present before the coverage took effect. For example, for the first 12 months, a disability plan may not cover a disability related to a medical condition that existed in the 3 months prior to being insured. After the 12-month period, the medical condition would be covered.

If Elena decides to leave her job, she should find out if all or part of the coverage can be changed or converted to an individual plan without providing proof of health, so that she can take it with her. If there are benefits that can be converted, she should consider the cost and any changes to the contract to determine if it is reasonable to pay the premium. Often the plans available to employees who leave a company have a higher premium and more restrictive benefits than what is available on the open market, so it is wise to contact an advisor to compare.

Group benefits are an amazing addition to your overall compensation package, but are often misunderstood and underutilized. Time frames for enrolling are frequently missed, which can significantly impact the availability and comprehensiveness of your plan. Benefits books can seem complicated, but it is worth the read to ensure you get the most out of your benefits plan.

TIP #8: Read your group benefits booklet, understand your plan, and don't miss the deadlines to enroll.

Chapter 9: Getting Hitched - Common-law or Marriage?

Ben and Julia have been living together for 2 ½ years. Ben has accumulated $15,000 in savings to put towards a down payment on a house. Julia recently finished school and does not have any savings. Since Julia didn't have any money to contribute to the down payment of the house they agreed that Ben would purchase the house and pay the mortgage payments and Julia would pay for expenses such as groceries, taxes and utilities. Ben purchased a home for $250,000. Unfortunately, they have recently decided to separate. The house is now valued at $300,000. Julia's name is not on title and she did not contribute to the down payment or the mortgage payments. As you can imagine, there are many questions that have come to light. Is Julia entitled to any equity in the house as part of the separation? Is she entitled to relief payments (also called dependency relief) from Ben if her income is not adequate to support her standard of living? From Ben's perspective, will he be required to forfeit part of the deposit he put down on the house and the equity accumulated in it? Will he have to provide financial support to Julia for a period of time?

The reality is that almost 50% of married or common-law relationships end in a breakdown and the laws pertaining to the entitlement to property and income relief vary from province to province. They also depend on whether the couple is married or common-law, and whether the area of law involved is estate law, tax law or family law. It's important to understand that the definition of what constitutes a common law relationship varies as well.

For example, if Ben and Julia lived in British Columbia, their common-law rights are the same as if they were legally married since they have lived common-law for over 2 years. In that case, the assets would be split equally and there would be a good probability for relief payments for a period of time if one of them made more money than the other. However, if they lived in Ontario or Nova Scotia, their common-law relationship would be recognized after one year for tax purposes, but under the rules of family law there is typically no built-in rights for the division of assets and little opportunity for relief payments.

While not a romantic proposition, especially at the beginning of a relationship, a cohabitation or marriage agreement may serve to protect assets and income in the event of a relationship breakdown. We recommend seeking legal advice to determine what is required in your jurisdiction.

The chart below provides a detailed outline of the different rights for married and common-law couples under estate and family law provisions in the province of Ontario. Please note that tax law recognizes a common-law relationship after 12 months, yet family and estate laws require 3 years before it is recognized with respect to dependent relief rights only.

Common Law Vs Marriage

	Definition in Ontario	Property Sharing in the event of relationship termination	Spousal Support in the event of relationship termination	Intestacy – passing away without a will	How to protect yourself
Common Law	Ontario Family Law Act: "Either of two persons who are not married to each other and have cohabited, (a) continuously for a period of **not less than three years**, or (b) in a relationship of some permanence, if they are the natural or adoptive parents of a child" The Ontario Succession Law Reform Act uses a very similar definition	No statutory rights to property accumulated during the marriage regardless of time or children together, or how "marriage-like" the relationship was unless the property is held in both names	Yes, after 3 years of living together, or if you have a child together	No statutory rights regardless of length of relationship, children, or how "marriage-like" the relationship was	"Cohabitation agreement" can be used to determine rights and obligations of each party during the relationship, in the event of a termination
Marriage	A formal union between 2 people as recognized by law	Spouses are entitled to an equal claim to property accumulated during the marriage, with some exceptions	Higher income spouse typically obligated to financially support the former spouse	Right to share in the estate of the deceased according to provincial succession line legislation. In Ontario, the first $200,000 of assets automatically goes to the surviving spouse; the rest is divided equally among spouse and children, if any	"Marriage contract" can be used to determine rights and obligations of each party during the marriage, and in the event of divorce

TIP #9: Understand the laws in your province regarding common-law and married relationships and ensure you have the proper paperwork in place to protect your income and assets.

Chapter 10: Just Do It! Wills and Powers of Attorney

You may wonder why you need a will, or have questions about when to get one. Although death is not likely to occur at a young age, it does happen. Since we are never completely in control of our own destiny, it is important to make sure your assets and your loved ones are protected.

A will is a document that outlines your wishes for the distribution of your property at the time of death, as well as who would become guardian of your children. If you die without a will it is referred to as being 'intestate', and provincial laws dictate who inherits your estate (assets), how much each individual will get, and who will look after your children. These laws may not reflect your wishes.

Like family and tax law, the rules of estate law vary from province to province. They also differ depending on whether a couple is married or living common law. For example, in Ontario, Quebec, New Brunswick, Nova Scotia, Prince Edward Island, and Newfoundland and Labrador, a common-law spouse is not recognized on intestacy in the same way as a married spouse. In Ontario, a married spouse receives a defined spousal distribution, even if the couple is separated at the time of death. This will happen even if the deceased is living with somebody else in a common-law relationship. The common-law spouse is not entitled to a share in the estate, although may be granted dependency relief through the courts. In Alberta and British Columbia, an eligible common-law spouse will receive the spousal distribution, and a married but separated spouse will receive nothing.

A Power of Attorney (POA) is a written authorization allowing someone to act on your behalf under certain circumstances. There are two types of POA, one for property and one for personal care. The POA for property provides authority for another person to handle your financial affairs in any situation when you are unable to act on your own behalf, for example, being incapacitated or travelling out of the country. A POA for personal care is only enacted when an individual becomes incapacitated and allows for decisions to be made regarding health and personal care. Again, the rules of eligibility vary between provinces.

It is important to have a will and POA's prepared by a lawyer and updated as major life changes happen. Life changes can impact the validity of the documents. For example, a will is nullified upon marriage but is typically not affected in the event of a divorce. It is also important to review your will and POA documents every 2-3 years.

Preparing a will and POA may seem overwhelming the first time you attempt to complete this task. Your lawyer will help guide you through the process.

TIP #10: Have a Will and POA and review and update them regularly.

The Wrap Up

We wrote this book to help you begin to build the foundation for future financial success by looking at some common financial pitfalls. It is by no means a replacement for individual sound professional advice. The best thing you can do to start yourself off on the right financial foot is build a team of trusted professionals to advise you. This should include an accountant, lawyer, investment and insurance advisor who work in collaboration with each other to help you meet your financial goals.

We hope this book makes you more confident and comfortable with financial decision-making, and helps you to prosper in your chosen careers and reach all of your financial goals.

If you would like more information, please contact us to arrange a meeting, or visit our website.

Our toll-free phone number is 1-888-347-2437, or you can email us at: info@zavitzinsurance.com

The 60 Minute Financial Guide
How to Thrive in Your 20s and Beyond

Building a good foundation for your financial future is critical. The hard part is in knowing how to avoid the common financial pitfalls people in their 20s often make. That's where we come in. We help people create financial road maps, which outline where you are now, where you are going and how to get there.

This book will take you from *thinking* you are doing the right thing to *knowing* you are doing the right thing. With it, you can take the necessary steps to help ensure your financial future is secure and develop the financial habits to do more than just get by—you can thrive.

If you want more information or just some advice, you can check out our website at www.zavitzinsurance.com or send an email to info@zavitzinsurance.com and we will take it from there.

If you found the book helpful, pass it along to your friends or email us and we will send them a free copy.

Follow us on

Twitter at @zavitzinsurance
Facebook www.facebook.com/zavitzinsurance
LinkedIN www.linkedin.com/company/zavitz-insurance-inc.

About the Authors

Terry Zavitz BMusA, CFP, CLU, CHS, GBA, EPC

Protecting families is the main reason Terry loves insurance. After 30 years in the business, Terry knows that disability and life insurance can make all the difference in the financial viability of a family in the event of death, disability or health changes. Her practice encompasses life and group insurance, but her true passion and expertise is in the area of Living Benefits. Zavitz Insurance Inc. is one of the larger independent disability insurance providers in Canada. Terry is a regular contributor to industry articles and speaks at events across the country.

Terry gives countless hours of her time to the community and is very active within her industry. She currently sits on the Board for London Health Sciences Foundation and is the co-chair of the Women's Health Campaign. She is one of the founders of the Financial Strengthening Program through Goodwill Industries Great Lakes and continues to actively manage the coaching element of the program. She is passionate about her industry and plays an active role in many associations, such as Advocis and CALU. Past activities include her roles as Chair of the Board of Advocis as well as the London Health Sciences Foundation, member of the Board of Directors for London Health Sciences Centre, and committee member at St. Joseph's Health Care, Merrymount Children's Centre, Orchestra London, and various other local organizations.

Terry is the recipient of the Queen's Diamond Jubilee Medal, the YMCA Women of Distinction award, and the Hopwood Award. Recently, Terry was inducted into the London Business Hall of Fame, honouring her dedication to her industry and community and also named as one of the Top 50 Women of Influence in Canada's Life Insurance Industry.

Our toll-free phone number is 1-888-347-2437 or you can email us at: info@zavitzinsurance.com

Justine Zavitz BComm, CFP, CHS, CLU

Justine graduated with an Honours Commerce degree from McMaster University and continued on to earn her Financial Planning Services diploma from Fanshawe College. She then decided to join the family business and became a full-time advisor.

Justine has continued to grow her insurance knowledge by obtaining the Certified Financial Planner (CFP), Certified Health Insurance Specialist (CHS) and Chartered Life Underwriter (CLU) designations.

Justine is actively involved in her community. She is a member of the Children's Health Foundation Ambassador Council and Young Professionals group, and the Bust a Move Steering Committee with St. Joseph's Health Foundation. She is a founding member of the Mentoring for Charity Golf

Tournament, which promotes mentorship between students and professionals in their field as well as a financial mentor for the Financial Strengthening Program at Goodwill Industries Great Lakes. She is the Chair for the Joe Dickstein Scholarship program, which was developed to support and encourage new advisors in the insurance and financial field.

Justine is also an active member of many professional associations and speaks at numerous events across the country. She serves on the Conference of Advanced Life Underwriters (CALU) Employee Benefits and Living Benefits Issue Group and was the youngest President of the London chapter of Advocis, a professional association for financial advisors.

In 2013, Justine was a recipient of London's Top 20 Under 40 award and in 2014, she was named one of the Top 50 Women of Influence in Canada's Life Insurance Industry.

Our toll-free phone number is 1-888-347-2437 or you can email us at: info@zavitzinsurance.com

www.ingramcontent.com/pod-product-compliance
Lightning Source LLC
Chambersburg PA
CBHW071008180526
45168CB00003B/1332